Buying a Home:

A Behind The Scenes Look At How The Mortgage Process Really Works

Copyright 2015

Tony Gillard

Table of Contents

Chapter 1

The 6 Most Expensive Mistakes Made by Homebuyers

I help people get into the largest debt of their life, and smile about it ☺

I want to start by sharing the most expensive mistakes made by homebuyers. Why? Because when you go to buy a home, these can cost *thousands of dollars.*

You need to be aware of these mistakes, because it's usually the same mistakes I see over and over again. And these mistakes can cost you a lot of money!

I have been a loan officer for over 12 years.

In my 12 plus years writing mortgages here in Oregon, I have seen these mistakes time and time again.

I do what I do because I love helping people buy homes! While the paperwork can sometimes be stressful, the joy of helping someone buy a home is very rewarding. It truly is an amazing job, and I feel blessed to be able to serve people in this career.

I wrote this book because I want you to be empowered to buy your first home, refinance your current home, or finally invest in your DREAM HOME!

To get started, here are the 6 most expensive and common mistakes I've seen here in Oregon.

These can cost you a lot of time and money...but they are completely preventable!

Expensive Mistake #1: Not Getting Pre-Approved

The first mistake people make is not getting "pre-approved."

Let me be clear: there is a difference between a pre-approval and a pre-qualification. Those are two entirely separate things!

Most of the frustration in buying a home can be traced to the confusion between these two terms.

Here's what these terms really mean:

A pre-qualification means that someone answers questions about their debts, income, and other relevant information. They might even bring in a pay stub to "prove" their income. But nothing is *officially* checked or documented.

A prequalification is going on the "honor system."

Based on the information given to them by the client, the loan officer will tell them if they would qualify for a home.....*in theory.*

This does NOT mean you are guaranteed to qualify.

Almost anybody can be prequalified, but an actual pre-approval requires more due diligence. A pre-approval is more "official" than a pre-qualification.

A common (and tragic) scenario is buyers going out to look at homes with a realtor because they are *prequalified*...but not *preapproved.* They think they are officially qualified to buy a home. But sometimes that's not true...

Maybe their debt to income is higher than they stated, because they forgot to mention a $500 car payment, or a $700/month child support commitment. Maybe they've only been at their job for a month, so there isn't enough official income history. Most of the time its not a result of the buyer being dishonest or exaggerating their income – it's because of the way lenders consider various types of income and expenses.

Take Donna the flight attendant as an example. A pretty straightforward scenario; she's a W2 employee of a major airline for the last 6 years and makes $54,000 a year. She has a small car payment and is carrying a $4,000 balance on her credit card. She said she just recently purchased the car and the car dealer said her credit was 740. At face value she seems a perfect candidate and qualifies nicely. However the difference between pre-qualify and pre-approve is in reviewing and verifying the application information with proper documentation. Upon reviewing Donna's tax returns it turns out that she writes off "un-reimbursed employee expenses" to the tune of about $9,000/yr AND she has a 'side business' of over priced smelly candles. It turns out that business isn't all that profitable and creates losses against her tax returns. Good for taxes; bad for getting a mortgage. Because of these two things, her qualifying income is reduced by nearly $1000/mo. This dramatically increases her debt-to-income and she doesn't actually qualify for the amount that a pre-qualification would indicate.

Whatever the reason, here's what you need to remember: a prequalification is NOT the same thing as an official pre-approval.

BEFORE YOU START HOUSE HUNTING, get a full pre-approval. This alone will prevent nine out of ten potential problems that come up during the financing process.

To put it in informal terms, a prequalification is like the loan officer saying, "Hey, we *hope* you qualify. It sounds like it should work if you're not lying to us with the numbers you provided."

Unfortunately, there are many variables that people just don't think of. This includes tax liens, a bankruptcy, child-support obligations, student loans, etc.

Okay Tony, So What Exactly Is A Pre-Approval?

Usually when someone calls and says, "Hi, I want to buy a house, I need to get pre-approved," I'll say, *OK, great. Let me get some information from you.*

This initial conversation is not official. It is not an actual pre-approval. It's a pre-qualification.

As a loan officer, I will find out information about their job, where they work, how much they work, what they make on a monthly basis...just the surface stuff. I want to gather a "big picture" perspective of your financial situation.

Depending on the answers I might say, "Based upon what you've told me, it looks like you would qualify to buy this house or a house in this price range."

Keep in mind at this point *I don't know their official credit score*—we're using the "honor system" here, and I'm trusting that what they told me is accurate!

During this phase, there is no "official documentation" of debts, income, etc. Basically, what we're trying to accomplish is finding out if it's worth it to move on to the next step.....*an actual pre-approval.*

Everything up to that point is just a pre-qualification.

Here's what an actual pre-approval looks like:

Pre-approval is where you will fill out an official application.

(Sometimes with pre-qualifications, you might fill out an application as well, as a way to get things started....it's just not binding)

This application will include your W2 forms for two years, your pay stubs, your tax returns for two years, and your entire credit report.

Then I find out your employment history.

How long have you been at your job?

"Oh, you're on commission income? OK, great. How long have you been receiving commission income?"

Here's why I need to know this info: if you have only been a commissioned employee for, let's say, six months, you can't use that commission income!

We usually require a two-year history of full time commission income.

Loan officers will sometimes just say, "Oh, you have commission income. Great. We're going to use that." However, it frequently happens that they don't do their due diligence....and the deal falls apart before closing because the commission couldn't be used after all.

Rather than avoiding the due diligence process, it's better to find out RIGHT AWAY if you'll qualify for your mortgage. If not, you'll be extremely disappointed that you didn't actually qualify for the home you wanted to buy. Your realtor will be upset, and the seller will be upset that you wasted their time!

The pre-approval process can seem intimidating, but it's not too complicated. Don't let it scare you. The bank just wants to make sure that they're making a good decision loaning you money! Especially after the last housing boom and bust, banks are extra careful to make sure they're making loans to creditworthy borrowers.

It might feel like they're trying to make you *not* qualify. And there's probably some truth to that. After all, you aren't borrowing $20,000 when you buy a house....usually you're borrowing ten times that amount—or more! So it makes sense that the bank would do some research to manage its risk.

If you pass the gauntlet, you're in.

The loan officer's job is to be the intermediary between the bank and the client. As your advocate, I WANT YOU TO QUALIFY.

As a loan officer, it's my job to find a way to make the deal work! I often view myself as a defense attorney presenting the strongest case to judge (lender) so that you are proven innocent!

Once you're approved, you're ready to go. You just have to wait for the right house to buy!

(Of course, if all of a sudden the house comes back with an appraised value of $30,000 less than your purchase price....then that obviously is a totally different scenario!)

Why You Might Not Get Pre-Approved (Even If You're Already *Prequalified*)

In my experience as a loan officer here in Oregon, there are some common reasons that a person might get prequalified….but not actually get *pre-approved*.

By far, the most common reason is that people aren't upfront about their financial situation.

Trust me—honesty is always the best policy! Remember the defense attorney analogy? Tell me all of your dirty laundry upfront so I know what I'm working with and can build the strongest case without surprised down the road.

It happens all the time that a person tells me their credit score is 720, but it's actually 650….or even 600. Obviously, this will effect whether or not this person gets pre-approved!

Sometimes I find that they have recently gone through a foreclosure or a bankruptcy that they "forgot to mention." This will definitely affect their creditworthiness.

Did you recently lose your job, or start making car payments on that new car you purchased?

This will alter your "debt-to-income ratio," which is a major part of how we calculate your ability to take on new credit.

Your debt-to-income ratio is your debt (all of the monthly payments that you pay on a monthly basis) compared to your monthly income. It's pretty self-explanatory.

For example, you tell me that you make $3,000 a month of income, and you have only $1,000 of debt payments. From a loan officer's perspective, that looks pretty good – that's a 33% debt-to-income (DTI) ratio.

But then I find out that you have an extra $600 in child support that you didn't disclose! Maybe you sincerely forgot to tell me that, or maybe you intentionally mislead me—the motive actually doesn't matter. The fact is, that's going to bump up your debt-to-income ratio to 53% and you're probably not going to qualify!

And that's why it's so important to be honest with your loan officer.

Tell us the truth! Once we know the truth, we can help you find a way to buy a home. If you hide your financial situation from us, it can create a nightmare and will likely result in a declined loan. By the way, if you think you have a way figured out to sneak something past the 'system', I guarantee its already been thought of; banks have been burned by it, and new guidelines and protections have been put in place to prevent it.

It is frustrating (and expensive) if you do not get pre-approved. You might waste a lot of time researching, driving around on Saturdays, looking online at listings, creating the vision in your mind of already living in and enjoying a home you find and ultimately making an offer on that home....only to find out that you aren't approved for the necessary loan.

That sucks! I hate it when this happens to my clients, and all I can say is "I told you so."

You should have gotten pre-approved before you started looking at homes.

And you should know that it infuriates your real estate agent, because they invest a lot of time, energy, and money working with you to help you find a home.

Many agents put 30,000-40,000 miles *a year* on their vehicles, because they're constantly driving their buyers around to show properties. That's a pretty hefty expense! Not a single agent I work with drives a Prius, even though they are quite popular here in Oregon.

A real estate agent's worst nightmare is finding out at the last minute that their client didn't qualify for a loan.

Because of this, all of the reputable agents I know require a pre-approval to get started. They usually won't even show you homes until you're <u>pre-approved</u>.

It's simply too risky to work with clients that aren't preapproved!

Here's the thing...

Ultimately, it's the real estate agent's reputation on the line.

Let's say you are a real estate agent who is representing a "pre-approved" buyer who wants to buy a house. They have made an offer and the seller accepted.

The seller's agent is thinking that they're going to sell the house, and the sellers believe that it's a done deal! But all of a sudden you get to the week before closing and it's revealed that the buyer doesn't qualify for the loan...

The agent and the seller that they represent will be outraged....

And rightfully so. They have lost out on opportunities to sell because the home was off the market for several weeks.

Things like that *should not happen.*

The buyers' agent will be equally frustrated because this should have been taken care of beforehand.

Ultimately, it's not the loan officer's fault if the client failed to disclose relevant financial information. However, if your loan officer didn't collect and verify the proper documentation, they are party to the problem.

This is also why credit reports are very important.

Credit reports provide more than just a score; they will reveal anything that could be forgotten or omitted that might torpedo a transaction (that's a technical term). The most benign things you would ever think of can cause delays or drama regarding your loan – things like consumer disputes or even errors on your report. You know, because you're Tim Johnson Jr. and you pay your bills on time, but your deadbeat dad Tim Johnson doesn't and his derogatory accounts were mistakenly associated with you. It happens more than you think.

Furthermore its important to understand that the 'free' consumer reports or reports that come with your credit card statement are simply a simulated score based on a couple key factors. These scores are not the result of the scoring model that the bureaus use nor are they ever inline with what a lender uses. These can be used as a guide especially as you may be working to improve your scores – but can only really be used to see the way in which your scores are trending.

Other documentation may also be necessary to help support/explain your overall financial picture. This includes things that sometimes happen in life, like divorce. If you've been divorced, child support documentation is extremely important. This will create a record of these expenses.

This gives the loan officer the ability to accurately assess your income, *so there are no surprises later on.*

In this hypothetical scenario, they will look at divorce decrees, support orders, and other possible documentation. A loan officer has to do their due diligence to ensure there are no surprises in underwriting!

We need to foresee any problems that could happen....before they happen so we can ensure your 'innocence' before the judge!

Expensive Mistake #2: Not Getting A Home Inspection.

If you do not get a home inspection before purchasing, this can be a financially fatal mistake.

A home inspection will show anything underneath the surface "research" of online photos and video and even the 'walk through'. The goal is to find out what needs to be repaired or fixed so there are no surprises later on (leaky roofs, damaged siding, cracked foundations, disrupted sewer lines, etc).

This is ESPECIALLY important in the somewhat damp climate like Oregon, where the not-so-tropical winters here often soak our entire state and last from October until the 4th of July.

A home inspection is the physical equivalent of a financial pre-approval.

Let's say you're looking at buying your first home...

You're walking through a listing with your agent and everything seems great. The floors look good. The walls look nice. You like the colors. The bathroom is updated, and the kitchen has newer countertops and brand new appliances. You think to yourself, "This is the one. This house is a home run!"

Did you stop to think about the *structural integrity* of the home?

Until you have an official home inspection, you're just looking at the surface. "I love this house. I love the rooms. I love the space. It'll be great for entertaining!" The emotional response that makes the new home buying process so fun.

That may all be true, but it's not going to be your dream home if you find out there is thousands of dollars of water damage, or that the roof needs to be re-shingled

ASAP. Sometimes you can't tell these things just by looking at them from the outside. It takes a trained professional to inspect the property to verify everything is legit—that's why we call it a home inspection. You need to resist the temptation to take uncle Bob's word for it or a friend that used to be in construction. It's important to use a licensed inspector because you won't be able to negotiate needed repairs without the report generated by a licensed inspector.

A home inspection will look deeper than the average person. Like a detective, a certified home inspector knows what symptoms might indicate there is a larger problem.

The inspector will look at the wiring and see if the wiring is outdated, or if there are any fire hazards. They will go up into the roof/attic and look at the shingles, vents, skylights, etc.

The inspector will also make sure there are no problems with rodents, mold, foundation, leaky pipes, roof damage, etc. They really get into the "nitty-gritty" of the house to make sure there are no issues.

I have seen the importance of this first-hand!

We had a homeowner claim that the roof was replaced 7 years ago, which sounded great. But once an inspector actually went up on the roof, they found some missing shingles that weren't visible from just standing in the front yard.

Now, I'm not saying the homeowner was lying, or trying to intentionally deceive the buyer. They probably had no idea! Regardless, hidden problems can and will create an *expensive* surprise to the homebuyer **if they don't have a home inspection.**

Its really common with new construction that people buying don't think an inspection and sewer scope is necessary – "it's brand new" they rationalize. The truth, I've seen more issues with new construction than with pre-owned homes. Often the builder is in a hurry to complete a project and many times the city/county inspector just go through the motions. In fact, a common occurrence is the plumbing of the home will be inspected when all of the pipes (sewer included) are exposed. The plumbing/sewer inspector from the county will sign off on the work completed, and then the construction crew will fill the trenches. I've seen extremely expensive problems resulting after this process; level issues that create problems with sewer back ups, broken pipes, etc. This is why getting an inspection is REALLY important, *especially* if the home is a new build.

Some Common Issues A Home Inspector Might Find

Based on my experience with clients, there are a few common things a home inspector will find that need to be addressed prior to closing.

They are not always expensive fixes, of course. Sometimes it's just a couple hundred dollars, or even less.

In older homes, plumbing is a very common and expensive issue to deal with. Especially here in Oregon, our plumbing lines have to deal with settling from rains and because we don't get the crazy long, harsh winters of the upper Midwest or East, often we are complacent. So when we do get a couple of days of frigid weather, all of a sudden we have plumbing and irrigation issues – because we didn't prepare! Many times these issues won't even present themselves until spring or early summer when we are excited to water the lawns without rain.

During a home inspection, leaky or damaged pipes can be discovered that otherwise weren't noticed by the homeowner. This could mean the costly project of replacing walls or ceilings if a pipe bursts....it would be better to invest the money in a home inspection up front (which usually just costs a couple hundred bucks).

Sometimes houses do not have proper drain systems set up....which means water in the basement come spring time. Again, you could prevent this problem with a proper home inspection.

The other thing to watch out for is any kind of mold. Mold is an *enormous* issue. It's hard to detect, so most people don't even realize they have mold in their homes. And let's face it, our climate tends to be mold's best friend.

However, just because there's a little bit of water condensation doesn't necessarily mean that there's mold!

The home inspector will go to the house and use a special tool that detects mold. Sometimes there is mold and a whole wall has to be replaced—the carpet, the baseboards, and everything else…..because it's a health hazard.

A very dangerous hazard.

Better to find out right away than have to deal with expensive renovations….or worse yet, getting sick!

And, to be clear, it's usually *not* the seller's fault. More than likely the seller didn't know, either.

This merely reinforces why I always encourage buyers to pay for a home inspection.

It will pay dividends long-term *and* short-term. And 'peace of mind' has its value too!

Now, that being said, home inspectors can't always find *everything*. Obviously, a home inspector can't just start punching holes in the walls to look at the wiring, or find out what's behind the walls.

When they look at the wiring, they look in the electrical boxes and do some tests. But they can't see behind the walls. They don't have X-Ray vision!

A home inspection can only go so far.

It's like buying a used car. You're going off of the fact that it looks good and you've been told it's good you may have even had a mechanic look at it, but you never know.

This is why it's really important to make sure that you work with a real estate agent that you trust.

A good agent is going to make sure that you're signing all the proper forms to help protect against any fraud or negligence.

If there's reasonable evidence to conclude that the seller had prior knowledge of a problem, there will be legal and financial protection for you.

I encourage buyers to always work with a reputable agent that is willing to fight for you. **If you haven't found a real estate agent yet, I will gladly refer you to one. I know many GREAT agents here in the Portland Metro and Southwest Washington area.** I've been working with Real Estate agents for over 12 years now (not counting the agent I used to buy my first home almost 20 yrs ago). I've found that the best agents and those I refer my clients to have the following 3 traits in common: 1. They put their clients needs & wants first – listening intently to understand what's most important and using that as the criteria to guide them throughout the process. 2. They communicate frequently and consistently throughout so that you are never left to wonder. 3. They are fierce negotiators! Make sure the agent you choose for such a large transaction exhibit the 3 qualities above.

Expensive Mistake #3: Not Caring About Anything But The Interest Rate On Your Loan

Some people choose which loan officer to work with solely based on who promised the lowest rates.

Instead of doing research into whether the loan officer knows what they are doing, a home buyer will just ask, "What's your rate?"

That's like walking into a car dealership and saying, "I don't care about the features. Just tell me what is the absolute cheapest car on this lot!"

Unfortunately, the interest rate is the easiest number to pay attention to. That's all you hear about on the news.

It's a metric most people can intuitively understand, so that's all they care about!

Interest rates. Interest rates. Interest rates are going up. Interest rates are going down. Interest rates this, interest rates that.

I'm here to tell you that there is more to the story than interest rates. Specifically, the "lowest interest rate."

I sometimes have clients who come in and say, "I saw someone on the Internet that said they can get me four percent."

Let me be brutally honest: if they can get 4% and another good loan officer is at 4.25% or 4.5%, that 4% *is probably too good to be true.*

Especially when it comes to mortgages, if it sounds too good to be true....it probably is.

You need to make sure that you're working with a loan officer who does their due diligence. Before quoting you rates and prices, they should know about your personal financial situation!

Not everybody qualifies for the same interest rates. There are several credit and financial criteria that factor into what rate you qualify for.

This is why you shouldn't pay attention to hype-filled advertisements online, on TV, or in newspapers. Usually these promote the "prime" rate, *a special interest rate for people with unusually great credit, that hold Platinum depository accounts with the institution that is quoting the rate and in many cases have fees associated with obtaining the 'too good to be true' rate that aren't immediately disclosed upfront.* Often these 'surprises' are unleashed after you've gotten too far along to switch.

Unfortunately, this makes great "bait and switch" advertising, so lots of mortgage companies promote their prime rate just to get people in the door.

Finding a loan officer you actually *trust* is much more important than finding the "lowest interest rate."

The problem solves itself—if you're working with a great loan officer, they will find you the best rate available based on your qualifications.

Just because your rate is 4% (or whatever the "prime" interest rate is) doesn't ensure your loan will actually close!

If you go with someone who says they can get a super low interest rate, you need to know that they're actually capable of closing the loan.

That's the whole purpose of this process.

You have to close! It wouldn't matter if the interest rate were *zero* if you can't close on the loan.

Sometimes loan officers are inexperienced (or they just need to make a commission, so they're desperate). They will do everything they can to get a loan closed, even if it's a shaky situation or they have yet to reveal their surprises.

But these sketchy deals might not close *on time.* That makes the sellers angry! It makes the sellers' agent unhappy, too. In a seller's market, it can also be the death of a deal. Most sellers in a hot market will have back-up offers, sometimes they are even better than the offer they accepted (supply, demand, competition, escalating offers). When a real estate transaction doesn't close on time you have to get an extension on the contract that is agreeable to the seller. If you were selling your home and the buyer went long and their loan officer seemed like they didn't know what they were doing, do you think its possible that you may take the offer that came in higher rather than extending? You bet!

Not only does it make everyone unhappy, it can be very expensive for you—the buyer.

You can lose a portion of your earnest money if this happens. You will also likely end up having to pay an extension fee for the rate lock.

This is why it's important to close *on time.*

I cannot stress enough that these problems can be avoided when you take the time to find a trustworthy loan officer....someone with *experience.*

And just to be clear, a loan officer isn't a salesperson. But the business model *is* based on commission. That's how loan officers get paid—a percentage of each deal.

They are often compensated based on loan volume or how many loans they close.

So there's always that hidden incentive of "just getting a deal done." Be aware of the incentives faced by loan officers.

Here's how you can tell if a loan officer really wants to help you, or if they're just trying to make a quick commission:

If you don't have a credit score that's high enough right now, a not-so-great loan officer might say, "Call me back in six months."

They do this because they want (or need) the immediate gratification of a closing. They want the deal to close right now because they want to go golfing or buy a new car. These loan officers aren't willing to invest time in helping you—they'll just move on to the next potential client that's ready to go right away.

A great loan officer is going to educate you about what you can do to raise your credit score so you can qualify to buy the home you want. *They go above & beyond to help and often have resources they can recommend or refer to help with credit repair and finance & tax planning.*

They will keep in contact with you and connect you with a good credit repair specialist and other professionals, who can help you raise your credit score.

In this way, the loan officer can help you achieve homeownership. That's the most important thing!

The loan officer wants what you want—*to get you in your home.*

A great loan officer thinks about how they can serve their clients long-term, not just the clients that are the "low hanging fruit" for easy commissions.

A great loan officer will help you get where you need to be financially—a mediocre loan officer will just take orders and process the paperwork.

A great loan officer is more of a teacher than a salesperson.

So if they're excitedly quoting you a lower rate than everyone else, just stop and think about it... It's not really a great rate if they can't deliver it.

You could probably go out and buy a used Hyundai for $5,000, but there's a reason a brand new BMW costs

$50,000. You can't manufacture the quality of a BMW for $5,000.

If you saw a new BMW advertised for $5,000, you would be correct in thinking....*Hmmmm, what's the catch?*

Without getting too deep into the financial theory of capital markets, what you do need to understand is that all the banks and mortgage companies are getting their resources from the same pool.

And that's the "pool" of global savings.

When you're borrowing money for a mortgage to buy a house, *it means that someone out there first had to save that money and lend it to the bank.* Before it's invested, capital first has to be created.

Most people call this "savings."

So if your mortgage company is promising a four percent interest rate—and everyone else is at four and a half—you have to remember that they're all getting the money from the same place.

If they're offering a completely different interest rate—everyone else is at 4.5% and they're at 4—there's probably a catch.

Mortgage interest rates are similar to gas station fuel prices—they're usually very similar, because the product (access to financial capital) is similar.

When there are noticeable price differences, it should alert you that *you're no longer comparing apples to apples.*

In almost every scenario I have ever encountered, a difference in interest rates cannot be explained by, "this company is simply a better deal." Almost EVERY SINGLE TIME there is a catch—some sort of fine print on the promotion that they're hoping you don't read.

Is there a hidden fee? A surprise coming in a couple years (such as an adjustable rate mortgage with an intro teaser rate)?

Remember: mortgage companies get their money from the same place. If a deal sounds too good to be true....it probably is.

Of course, there will always be a minor difference in rates amongst competitive companies, but if one company quotes a number that's not aligned with other quotes.....you should always read the fine print!

The interest rate is not the most important thing.

The most important thing is the expert service that your loan officer provides, and the firm expectation that your loan will close, ON TIME.

In the short-term, there can be variances in interest rates (some companies have their assets allocated a little bit differently). It's not as if all mortgage companies are *always* going to be 5%, 5.5%, 7.25%, etc. That just reflects the various efficiencies of those firms.

I don't want to scare you by saying a low quote should be a "red flag," but you should always proceed with caution. Do your due diligence!

Expensive Mistake #4: Not Looking At The Total Cost Of Being A Homeowner

Another factor that a lot of buyers don't look at is the total costs of homeownership.

It's not just your principal and interest payment.

You have to take into consideration your property taxes, homeowner's insurance, potential HOA fees, utilities, and miscellaneous expenses like general wear and tear, or a capital reserve fund (for spendier fixes like a new roof, siding, etc).

All these things can really add up!

If you have a large lawn, you have to buy a lawnmower when you move in...or pay somebody to mow your lawn if you don't buy a lawnmower. This can add $50 a week just in lawn maintenance. Is the lawn *really* big? You might need a riding lawnmower.

Did you budget for that?

You don't want to buy a house that makes you "house-poor," meaning the expenses overwhelm you every month.

This may sound obvious, but some people pay a flat rate for their rent, which includes utilities. Are you prepared to pay for your monthly utilities like water, cable, electric, etc?

If you're living with Mom and Dad, maybe your utilities are paid for. Are you ready to take on that responsibility for yourself?

There are a lot of real estate companies now—whether it's an apartment complex or even single-family homes—where the rent is higher but all of your utilities are covered.

The landlord just charges a flat rate to keep things simple.

You may pay the utilities in your apartment, but paying for utilities in an apartment building versus a single-family home can be a shock to some people. In an apartment, you benefit from structural and financial efficiencies. You don't have this advantage when you're paying to heat/cool your own home.

For some people, this can seem overwhelming.

If you're used to paying $1,000 a month in rent but most of your utilities are taken care of, there's a pretty good chance that your apartment building is extremely efficient.

If you think you can afford $1,000 a month mortgage, you might be completely forgetting that utilities alone could be $200-$400 a month.

Especially in a WET state like Oregon....we have something called rain and moss and leaves. There are other expenses to consider – like GUTTER CLEANING or roof maintenance.

If that's something that you didn't plan for...

The solution is simple....*plan for it!* A great loan officer will help you with this plan! They will help you build a budget and determine your true buying power based on your specific circumstances.

Expensive Mistake #5: Not Considering Future Financial Needs When Choosing A Mortgage

Another important distinction is to *get the right mortgage for YOU.*

Some people come in to my office and tell me, "I want a 15-year mortgage because I'm going to pay it off right away," or, "I have a lot of extra cash flow right now."

They probably recently read a book by Dave Ramsey, or one of the other famous anti-debt gurus. For the record, usually these financial experts give great advice! This only problem is that financial advice is not a "one size fits all" prescription. Everybody's situation is different.

The best way to pay off a house is....

Well, that's assuming there is only one "best way" to pay off a house!

Most of my clients that come in with that mindset end up going with a 30-year mortgage (because the interest rates are not that different right now).

This gives them better cash flow every month (lower payments). Not only right now, but in the future.

If they have a daughter's wedding they have to pay for, college tuition, investments like a 401K, medical emergencies, etc., they will have the peace of mind *and the practical ability to access money when they need it.*

When you have a lower monthly payment, this gives you the freedom to choose to pay more on the loan if you want to. It's a win-win. Even the tax benefits are stronger with a 30 yr mortgage than with a 15 yr mortgage.

Incidentally, there are usually no penalties to pay off a loan early.

Especially with interest rates where they're at right now, **you have to think about the opportunity cost of your capital.** If you're paying a mortgage payment that's only 3% on a shorter-term loan, could you have invested the difference for more than 3%?

Probably!

If you pay it down early, it's the same thing as investing your money for a 3% return. That's the "opportunity cost."

Paying a mortgage that's a nine percent interest rate is the equivalent of investing your money at a 9% return. Of course, rates aren't at nine percent yet.....but historically, that's almost normal!

This book is being written in 2015. Maybe you're reading this book in 2017 and rates are 10 percent. If you paid on your mortgage at 10 percent, it's the same thing as investing your money for 10 percent.

The concept of "opportunity cost" comes from the field of economics. In a nutshell, all prices are a form of opportunity cost. *Everything is inexpensive or expensive relative to what else you could have bought for the same amount of money.*

What opportunities are you giving up by having a 15-year mortgage?

(I don't mean to scare you out of a 15-year mortgage. I just want you to be clear on *why* you're making your decision)

If your payments are going to be higher with a 15-year mortgage or a 20-year mortgage, what's the opportunity cost of how you otherwise could have used that money?

Now, in some cases, it absolutely makes sense to do a 15-year mortgage. I'm not trying to discourage folks from doing that. Just consider the big picture!

Many people take a 15-year mortgage *that should have went with a 30-year mortgage.*

The inverse is not true.

Look at the options, and choose what's best for you. Usually, you'll be able to make the right decision once you've talked with an experienced loan officer. I'd be happy to help!

Remember: just because you want a shorter loan (to save on interest) doesn't mean you can't get a 30-year mortgage and simply pay it down faster.

The desire to pay down the loan quickly is the primary reason why people want a shorter term....but there are usually other, better ways to accomplish this!

It's the loan officer's job to help you make an informed decision. Being empowered with the necessary knowledge is a great feeling!

The person with options is the person with freedom.

Here is the bottom line: if you don't know whether a 15-year or 30-year mortgage is right for you, *you are going to pay a lot more total interest with a 30-year mortgage.*

That being said, you will have more options when you spread those payments out over 30 years. Your monthly payments will be considerably smaller and your tax benefit will be larger which gives you more financial flexibility.

Managing your cash flow is really, really important!

If something happens unexpectedly, like a car accident, a $10,000 new roof, maybe some unexpected water damage in your basement....what will you do?

A couple years ago during the "Great Recession," many people lost their jobs. Are you prepared to weather another economic storm like that?

What will you do if that happens again?

This is why it's important to factor in your *cash flow sensitivity* when choosing a mortgage. How much margin do you have every month? You don't want to cut it too close. That's a recipe for disaster.

If you don't have a mortgage payment that uncomfortably stretches your monthly finances, you will enjoy life with more peace of mind.

A 30-year mortgage can free you up to save some money so you have a "safety net." As I've said, it's all about the opportunity cost!

Consider these things when choosing which mortgage product is right for you. A 30-year isn't automatically best, a 15-year isn't automatically best, adjustable rate isn't automatically best, and a fixed rate isn't automatically best.

Look at the long-term consequences, and choose the mortgage that will help you accomplish your financial goals.

Here's the best question to ask yourself: which mortgage product will give me the most options? Because the most important thing is having options!

You want flexibility. A cushion.

A good loan officer will review all the options with you, and how they would affect your financial goals and explain the pros and cons of each – paying special attention to what is most important to you!

Two Types of Loan Officers: The Difference Between Order-Takers and Advisors

Some people have the impression that a loan officer is just a glorified *order taker*—nothing more than a fast food cashier that happens to be selling mortgages, not burgers.

"Oh, they're just going to take my papers and shuffle them around, type some stuff into their software, and then the software will automatically tell them what I qualify for."

Unfortunately, like any profession, there are always bad apples. But the true professionals go far beyond the role of an "order taker."

A great loan officer is a true *advisor*.

A great loan officer is like a teacher that can guide you throughout the process. They don't simply do "the work," they make a proactive effort to keep you informed on the timeline and progress of things. And beyond the transaction management, *they coach you to make an empowered financial decision.*

If your loan officer isn't doing this, find a new loan officer. This is often one of the largest financial transactions that you will ever encounter - you deserve more than an order taker!

The value created by a great loan officer isn't the *information* they give you, or even the *knowledge* they share with you about how the mortgage process works. The real value is a third step beyond information and knowledge....*wisdom.* Is your loan officer sharing their wisdom with you, so you can benefit from their years of experience?

(If all a loan officer does is punch in the required numbers, they will soon be replaced by basic software that automates this process)

Just like a realtor does more than showing homes, a loan officer should do more than just "shuffle paperwork," as I've overhead people colloquially phrase it.

So, what should you expect from your loan officer? What are the specifics you should look for?

You want to find someone who is not rushing you.

As a homebuyer, you'll want to look for someone who takes his time to meet with you in person, or listens intently, gives you their undivided attention, and walks you through the steps of becoming a homeowner.

This can be an intricate and complicated process—many loan officers suffer from what's called the **"Curse of Knowledge."** They've been through the process so many times that they've forgotten how complex it can seem to their clients.

They take for granted how much they know, so they tend to rush things. This creates unnecessary stress for the client—and the last thing a real estate transaction needs is more stress!

A great loan officer takes the time to explain everything and communicates often, *so the client always feels in control of the situation.*

For most people, it's unnerving to work with a loan officer who just says, "I need these documents from you. Sign them and I'll contact you later."

Remember, this is probably the largest purchase of your life.

You won't feel very comfortable walking out the door when someone just shuffled you out of their office to get to the next person. You should never feel like a product on a mass assembly line.

Here's how this *should* work: after searching for homes online for a couple weeks, you finally contact a loan officer to get the house hunting process started. You agree to meet at their office or discuss your situation over the phone so you can start the preapproval process. When questions arise about why they need your paystubs, or why you can't use irregular commissions as proof of income, your loan officer is happy to explain the reasoning behind these policies. They calmly explain to you how the process works, and why some forms of documentation are required. Furthermore, they coach you throughout this process to find a win-win solution. Real estate often happens after business hours – after you clock out for work. So make sure your loan officer can take calls after hours and on weekends.

The difference here between a mediocre loan officer and a great loan officer is that a great loan officer doesn't just tell you the bad news (if there is bad news).

They always help you find *the solution.*

They go beyond information and knowledge—their most important deliverable is *wisdom.*

A great loan officer goes above and beyond simply "doing the paperwork." A great loan officer takes an active role in *mentoring* the client and presenting the best 'case' to the underwriter to ensure approval.

Let's be honest: mortgages are boring. Most people are not experts in financing residential real estate...nor do they want to be! *They just want to buy a home.* A loan officer bridges this gap of boredom, frustration, and fear....so the client can buy the home of their dreams.

When it comes time for YOU to buy a house, make sure you work with a loan officer that's a true advisor.

Expensive Mistake #6: Not Being Upfront About Your Numbers

This should be common sense...

Unfortunately, it is not.

One of the dumbest, most EXPENSIVE mistakes I see over and over again is trying to "fudge the numbers."

Some people take creative liberty when describing their financial situation to the loan officer, hoping the loan officer won't find the truth.

People will exaggerate their income by $1000/month, or "forget to disclose" debts they are liable for. It's usually not the obvious things that will get you in trouble, because most people are smart enough to realize they can't "hide" a $400/month car payment.

It's the not-so-obvious items that are easy to rationalize as minor, unimportant expenses.

Most people won't outright lie on their applications or documentation, but they will use their creativity to make their financial situation seem better than it actually is.

This is tempting for one reason: it buys you time. Rather than confronting the reality of your finances right now, you confront it later on.

Unfortunately, in real estate as in life, honesty is the best policy.

If you get "lucky" after fudging some numbers (I would argue *unlucky*), and your loan application moves towards a closing date….you won't be so lucky at closing.

Don't do it…*it's just not worth it.*

Not only will a botched closing be embarrassing, it will infuriate your real estate agent, the seller's agent, and your loan officer. These professionals have invested dozens of hours on your transaction, and you were misleading them the whole time. It's not fair to you, and it's not fair to them.

Be completely upfront about your financial situation if you want to have a good, solid peer approval.

This includes your income AND your expenses!

Maybe you're not sure that you can use your overtime income—it would be best to approach the application process as conservatively as you can. Tell your loan officer the *truth*.

Here's the one sentence you need to remember: if they know the truth, your loan officer can help you get what you want. If you mislead them, they are helpless to help you.

Potential "surprises" could be tax liens, using child support for income, using overtime pay rates, or using commission-based income that doesn't have a proven consistency.

Please, please, please... disclose it! When in doubt, tell the truth. **If your loan officer knows the truth, they can help you get what you want. If you mislead them (or withhold relevant information), they are helpless to help you.**

As loan officers, we want to help you. We want to help you move into the home of your dreams. We are here for you. We are cheering for you! *We are on your side.* Remember the analogy of the attorney/client relationship? Have you ever seen Matlock or Perry Mason get sideswiped because their client 'forgot' to tell them something damaging....only to have it turn up

Chapter 2

The Most Important Decision You Make When Buying A Home (It's Probably Not What You Think)

Why is choosing a realtor so important?

Because everything that goes into buying a house— touring homes, finding the perfect neighborhood, the offer strategy, negotiation with sellers, advising best inspections, handling the contract legalities and ensuring your protection—will be managed by your agent.

You will always be in control, but your agent is managing the process. They are your advisor. If you choose a great advisor, everything will work smoothly. If you choose a not-so-great advisor, you are setting yourself up for failure.

At the risk of hyperbole, I want to make a bold statement: if you pick a great realtor, you can make a lot of mistakes throughout the process, and it will still work out in the end. Therefore, you should use your mental energy choosing an awesome realtor, and then trust them to guide you through the process.

Don't worry about the details—your realtor will be there to answer your questions.

If you're worried about the time commitment (and stress) of the home buying process, do yourself a favor: simplify things by focusing on just ONE DECISION.

The one decision you need to research is which real estate agent to trust. *That's it.*

Almost every other decision flows from this prerequisite.

And by the way, as a buyer, the agent you use is FREE…. So you might as well pick the best one!

A great realtor, by definition, is someone who can use their years of experience to make sure their clients get what they want (even if the client isn't sure what that is).

The one mistake you cannot afford to make is choosing the wrong real estate agent.

If you choose the right agent, almost nothing can stop you from finding a home you love. If you choose the wrong agent, almost anything can stop you.

There are dozens of decisions that go into buying a home. Don't worry about it! Focus on one thing at a time. Specifically, that "one thing" should be finding an awesome agent.

Don't stress about finding the perfect neighborhood, your list of must-haves, your perceived budget, your timing, your offer strategy (if you're in a competitive seller's market), or anything else that may come up.

You will soon encounter *decision fatigue*, and you'll start to make poor, rushed choices. This is why you need a realtor. When you work with an experienced agent, the only decision that requires research and due diligence is choosing the right agent in the first place.

Once you find an agent you can trust, they will mentor you throughout the process.

Here's an analogy: you are the "CEO" of the transaction. Your realtor is the VP that manages the day-to-day operations. They handle the details; you are responsible for the big picture "vision."

Don't let yourself get caught up in the stressful details. Let your real estate agent worry about that stuff—that's why you pay them a commission. Well, they get paid by the seller…. But you know what I mean.

A good real estate agent is someone who's going to work for you, stand up for you, explain things to you, and make sure that you are fully aware of the entire process, throughout the entire process.

They will make sure that they're getting you the very best deal.

From a loan officer's perspective, a good realtor is someone who has experience, and someone who is *familiar with the mortgage process.*

Unfortunately, one small mistake can blow the whole deal up. That's why it's so important to work with a loan officer and a real estate agent that you TRUST.

You should do just as much research finding a real estate agent as you do finding a house.

(This is the opposite of what most people do.)

The Characteristics I Personally Look For In Finding A Real Estate Agent For My Clients

If I have a client that isn't yet working with a realtor (or maybe working with a friend of the family that does hair as their full time occupation) there are a few non-negotiables of what I expect *before* I refer a client.

- I want them to be professional (not a part-time hobbyist).
- I want them to be experienced.

- I want them to have amazing communication and transaction management skills.

If I could narrow all of this down to one thing, the most important characteristic in a real estate professional (loan officer or agent) is their *communication skills.*

I am constantly communicating with my clients, probably *over-communicating*. My agents sometimes email me, "You don't need to contact me so much."

This is actually a good thing—I would rather err on the side of *over-communication.* Unfortunately, this is the OPPOSITE of what most real estate professionals do.

Many real estate professionals are completely lacking in communication skills. They forget that this business isn't just about houses or interest rate percentages….it's about *people.*

I am always sending out emails, texts, phone calls, video updates (whatever my clients prefer), and making sure the client knows what's going on.

If the client is not aware at all times of the status of the transaction, the loan officer and/or real estate agent is failing at their job.

Imagine you're with your friends on a Friday night and they ask about "how things are going with your new home."

You're super excited, but you tell them the truth. "I have no idea. I haven't heard from my agent or my loan officer in a while."

As a buyer, that's a frustrating and an anxious place to be.

The truth is fear comes from not knowing (fear of the unknown) so the more time that goes by that you don't get updates, the more fear arises. "Is everything ok?", "Are things still moving forward?", "Should I start planning for the move or should I wait?" It only takes a quick phone call every week to keep your clients updated! As a buyer, you should expect *weekly communication.* Once the process moves forward, the frequency of communication should increase.

I would never refer a client to a realtor just because they're in the same city. This is probably the most common mistake—choosing the real estate agent based on *convenience.*

It's far better to do some independent research, and get recommendations from people you trust.

Ask the real estate agent to provide references from the last two or three clients they worked with. Not just two or three references in general, *but the most recent clients they worked with.*

(This will prevent them from cherry picking success stories, and give you a more accurate preview of what they're like to work with)

PS

This is such a critical part of the process and a major component in a successful transaction – I can't stress the importance of a great agent enough. As a loan officer here in Oregon and SW Washington, I've had the privilege of working with some AMAZING real estate agents. **I'd be more than happy to connect you with an agent I trust with client testimonials to back it up.** Email me at: *tony@mymortgageguytony.com* if even to interview them and compare their experience and service philosophy with someone you may have already began working with.

Chapter 3

The Truth About Down Payments: How Much Will I Actually Need To Save Up?

A lot of people have questions about down payments.

In fact, most people reading this book will skim through the table of contents, and then immediately skip to this chapter.

If you're house hunting, you're probably wondering:

- Can I really buy a house with no money down?
- How much money does someone realistically need to buy a house?
- What are the requirements right now for down payments?
- Will I qualify for the government programs?
- Do all homes qualify for down payment assistance?

While I can't answer all of these questions without knowing the specifics of your situation, let's start with the basics.

First off, *it is not 2004 anymore.*

In 2004 (or any of the so-called "housing boom" years of the new millennium), the market conditions were totally different.

For example, there are many articles, books, and programs being sold that teach people how to be a real estate investor. They make it sound really easy, *because they want you to buy their high-priced educational program!*

Long story short, it was much easier to qualify for a home in 2004 than it is today. Lending standards were very relaxed in those years, which is why so many people made the leap from renting to owning.

In today's market, there are stricter standards for documentation. You can't just walk into a bank, tell them how much you make, and then instantly qualify for a mortgage.

Compared to the regulatory environment of today's real estate industry, the past twenty years seem like the Wild West!

Times have changed. Government regulations are much different, *although many of the same programs are still in place.*

When someone asks me a general question like, "How much do I really need for a down payment," I have to remind them that this is a rather open-ended question. The honest answer is....*it depends.*

Of course, this isn't what the client wants to hear. They want to know what they'll qualify for...and they want to know *now.*

I guess that's just a consequence of living in our "instant-access" culture. We want to stream videos, *instantly.* We use Google to find information, *instantly.* We use DVR to record our favorite shows so we can watch them, *instantly*. Except for me…. my kids set a timer for Sponge Bob and apparently there was a Sponge Bob marathon…. my DVR is full – no room for my shows. But for the most part, life in the 21st century is all about instant gratification (think microwave popcorn).

Unfortunately, navigating the regulatory and financial requirements for mortgage qualification is not as simple as punching in a couple numbers and hitting START.

There's not a one-size-fits-all answer to a vague question like *How much do I need for a down payment?*

There are many different programs and qualification requirements.

For instance, on a "conventional" loan (which usually requires higher credit scores), most people think *you have to put 20 percent down.*

Let me be very clear: you do NOT have to put 20 percent down to buy a house.

If you don't want mortgage insurance, you will have to put 20 percent down. However, this is a huge misconception that's misunderstood by the public.

You don't NEED to put 20% down. AND, mortgage insurance isn't the EVIL that most people have been trained to believe that it is.

You can put as little as 3 percent down and still be able to buy a home. The details will depend on the specifics of your situation.

So...what is "Mortgage Insurance?"

In a nutshell, *mortgage insurance* is insurance for the lender in the event that you go into default.

There is more risk involved with a higher loan to value (LTV) loans. Someone that puts 5% down to buy a home is more likely to default than someone who puts 20% down to buy a home. This is statistics – not a character assault. The smaller the down payment, the less "skin in the game" you have as a borrower. Lenders want to align your incentives with theirs.

In short, the less money you put down, the more risky the loan is (statistically). Naturally, they need to hedge their risk...which is why they require you to pay mortgage insurance.

It's the same reason you carry car insurance—of course, you never plan on getting in an automobile accident. That's why it's called an *accident*. But just in case, you pay for car insurance to protect against a *possible* accident! In the same way, you never plan on defaulting on your mortgage. But just in case, the lender wants to have insurance on that loan.

Usually, once you hit 80 percent loan-to-value or below (which would be the case if you put down 20 percent), you would not have to pay mortgage insurance. There are different criteria that you have to meet in order to remove mortgage insurance – this will depend on the program and the way in which you reached 80% loan-to-value or below. These are important matters to discuss with your loan officer during the planning and pre-approval stage.

Most people do not put 20% down, so they do pay mortgage insurance.

So the obvious question becomes...how much does mortgage insurance cost? Of course, this is an open-ended question also. It depends on the loan program, the loan amount, your credit score, your debt to income and on the loan to value (the loan amount versus you're the value of the home), etc.

However, I can say with certainty that it varies a lot from one program to the next. FHA programs for example have higher mortgage insurance factors but their rates are subsidized and are often below market. Conventional mortgage insurance factors are more dependent on credit scores than FHA. USDA mortgage insurance factors are quite low and VA doesn't require mortgage insurance at all. It's important that your loan officer compare all programs so you can see side by side the difference, discuss the pros and cons of each with your loan officer and choose what program is best for you.

With current market conditions, I would guesstimate that for a typical $250,000 house mortgage insurance is going to range from $40/month to $170/month. Again, this range is affected by program, down payment amount, credit score and debt to income. *Of course, these statistics could change by the time you're reading this book.* Please contact me if you want accurate information for YOUR situation. And always keep in mind that the "mortgage calculators" that you will find on various websites rarely include mortgage insurance. If you are not careful in estimated the total cost of a home including the down payment and the total monthly payment, you may be looking at homes that are outside of your budget.

Mortgage insurance is not something that's going to be an extra $20 a month. It's certainly not a minor expense.

You need to budget for it.

A good loan officer is already going to figure this out for you. They will find out what kind of down payment you *want and need.....for YOUR situation.*

I know it might sound cliché, but everyone's situation is different. One program might be a perfect fit for a client, but that same program isn't the best option for another client. Mortgages are not a one-size-fits-all product category. It takes an expert advisor to help you navigate this process.

Find a loan officer you can TRUST.

The Most Common Mortgage Programs

What are your options when it comes to down payments? What are your options for structuring the monthly payments? Let's unpack the options you may have by looking at the most common mortgage products. This is NOT an exhaustive list of programs that are available – which is why it's important to work with an advisor with experience and access. Bigger banks usually only have a couple programs that they can provide whereas a banker/broker will have much broader access to many mortgage programs.

Conventional Loan

With conventional loans you can go as low as three percent down. A conventional loan is a "conforming" loan, so the maximum loan amount is $417,000. As an example, a purchase of $438,000 with 5% down would be an amount borrowed of $416,100 and would qualify as a conventional mortgage. Anything above $417,000 is considered a "jumbo" loan amount. Jumbo loans will often require a larger down payment and higher credit score requirements.

The minimum credit score for a conventional loan is 620; however the rate on conventional loans are 'risk based' which means the better your credit score the better the rate that you will qualify for. Often when your score is less than 680, an FHA mortgage will make more sense. The following credit tiers show the 'cost' differential for credit scores ranging from 620 to 740+

Representative Credit Score	
≥ 740	0.000%
720 – 739	0.250%
700 – 719	0.750%
680 – 699	1.250%
660 – 679	2.000%
640 – 659	2.500%
620 – 639	3.000%

This means that for a $200,000 mortgage loan a borrower with a credit score of 680, any given rate will cost the borrower 1.25% of the loan amount or $2500 more than a borrower with 740+ credit scores.

Here's what you need to know: most of these are *guidelines* rather than legal rules. A good loan officer will guide you through this process so you don't get intimidated. They will also discuss the various programs that you qualify for and help you determine the best solution based on your individual and unique needs.

Usually, people who use conventional loans have established credit, are often successful business owners, move-up buyers, professionals who already have financial credit established and even some first time home buyers that have been very responsible with their bills. They will have money set aside for the potential down payment, and be generally familiar with the process.

What are the advantages of a conventional loan?

Right now the biggest advantage is the mortgage insurance. If you're not putting 20 percent down, the mortgage insurance premium on a conventional loan is *less* than an FHA loan and will come off when you reach a certain loan to value.

(This is because FHA loans are often riskier than traditional loans from the lender's perspective)

FHA loans have a lower interest rate because it is subsidized by the government, but the mortgage insurance is higher….and it's permanent mortgage insurance - for the life of the loan.

This is not so with conventional loans.

It's common sense: with less risk, there are less "risk premiums" to pay for as the borrower.

Disadvantages Of A Conventional Loan

One of the main disadvantages of conventional loans is the debt-to-income ratio threshold is a little bit lower.

The debt-to-income ratio is the amount of debt you have versus your income.

Lenders look at this two ways – so there are two qualifying numbers. The front-end ratio (which is your housing expense alone as a percentage of your income); and the back-end ratio (which is your housing expense plus any other monthly liabilities as a percentage of your income). 'Other liabilities' include things like car payments, credit card minimum payments and student loan payments (even if they are in deferment).

For example, if you have $150/mo of school loans, $200/mo minimum credit card payments and a $450/mo car payment you have a total of $800/mo in liability payments before housing expense. If you earn $60,000/yr ($5,000/mo) your ratio before housing expense is 16%. Conventional loans have a max 43% back end ratio which means 43% of $5,000/mo or $2150/mo is the max of total monthly liabilities ($800) + housing expense (total mortgage payment cannot exceed $1350/mo).

What does this mean for the average buyer?

Well, it means that your debt-to-income ratio has to be 43 percent or below without having to go to an "exception."

You can go up to 45 percent, but you have to have some *compensating factors.* Lenders like to keep it at 43 percent.

Don't worry, I'll explain all of this lender jargon!

Here's another example. Let's say you're a public school teacher making $40,000 a year.

If you're a public school teacher making $40,000 a year, and you have consistent job history, you'll want to keep your total housing payment (plus other debts) below 43% of your monthly income.

In this case, $17,200/yr ($1433/mo) of debt would keep you at a 43% debt-to-income ratio. This would include your new housing payment plus any other monthly liabilities (like car payments and credit card payments).

As a guideline, this means **your total housing payment + monthly debts should not exceed 43 percent of your gross monthly income.**

Again, you can sometimes go beyond that, but a lender would like to keep it at or below 43 percent.

The benefit of having a lower ratio is that it lowers the perceived risk, so you'll get the best interest rate too!

Obviously, the average person buying a house makes more than a thousand dollars a month. But just for the ease of the math, that means for every $1,000 of income you have, your total debts cannot exceed $430-$450.

With FHA, your ratio can go up a little bit higher because it's government backed, *but you're going to pay a premium for that.*

There is no free lunch.

You're going to pay a higher amount of mortgage insurance on your FHA mortgage. Also, with FHA loans, you pay an upfront mortgage insurance premium; you pay 1.75 percent of your total loan amount *upfront*. This is the FHA funding fee that helps fund the program.

It is rolled into the loan, so it's not an out of your pocket expense. But it does go on to the life of your loan, so you're still paying it either way.

You can have a much higher debt-to-income ratio than conventional, sometimes even 56 percent on FHA.

Alternatives To Conventional Loans

Of course, there are many people who do not qualify for a "conventional" loan! If you are in this situation, let's talk about the alternatives.

With a conventional loan, you could come in with 20 percent, or as low as 3 percent for the down payment.

However, many people don't have the necessary savings to put 20% down. That can be a lot of money!

Here are your options:

1. FHA Loan

A loan through the FHA (Federal Housing Administration) is one option that I touched on earlier in this chapter. Basically, it's a government-backed loan via the Federal Housing Administration. This federal agency exists in part to subsidize mortgages for homebuyers, so the "American dream" is more affordable.

If you do qualify for the loan, the FHA loan requires a 3.5% down payment.

On a $200,000 house, this means we're talking about a $7,000 down payment.

Before 2008, people would choose this option almost every time. 3.5% sounds a lot better than 5%, down, right?

Well....the truth is a little more complicated.

Mortgage insurance premiums have increased a considerable amount over the past few years. FHA has decided that it's a permanent requirement of the loan for the entire length of the loan term (30 years).

Meaning: *the mortgage insurance is not going away*.

With FHA, you could put 30% down and the loan will still require a mortgage insurance premium!

And for most homebuyers, this is not an insignificant expense: it can be a hundred dollars plus per month.

You should also know that FHA loans are NOT specifically for first time homebuyers.

There is a lot of confusion on this issue, because a lot of advertising is directed at first time buyers. People automatically assume that this program is only for first time buyers, which is not true. *Almost anyone can use an FHA loan.*

The most common reason that a first-time homebuyer will use an FHA loan is simply because it requires a low down payment, somewhat less restrictive guidelines and the rate isn't risk based (or credit score driven).

Gift As Down Payment

A little known fact is that you can actually use a gift for your down payment. Say you have a grandfather who wants to give you some help. If you were purchasing a $200,000 home, he could give you a gift of $7,000 and you would be able to use that for the down payment.

Of course, not everyone has someone in his or her life that will give them this kind of gift, but it is a possibility to consider.

Both FHA and conventional loans allow for gifts to be used as the down payment.

In general, you don't necessarily need to have earned the money to save for your down payment. *You just need to be able to verify where it came from.*

If you have a rich uncle that wants to give you $10,000 as a Christmas gift…you can use that as long as you can "source it." Lenders will want documentation!

TIP: If you want to avoid the paper trail from the donor to you, make sure to have the gift deposited > than 60 days before taking loan application.

Otherwise you have to have paperwork to show where the money came from – gift letter from donor, donor's bank statements, transaction history of the gift from the donor and from your account showing it going in.

3. First Time Home Buyer Programs

As I mentioned earlier, FHA is not necessarily a first time homebuyer loan. People probably have heard the phrase, "The first time homebuyer program."

There is no singular *first time buyer program*. This is a general term for many different programs.

It's important for your loan officer to discuss with you your objectives, what is most important to you and how the programs that are available – and more importantly the programs that you qualify for, will be best suited to achieve your goals.

4. Rural Development Program

If you've ever heard someone mention the "RD" program or "USDA loan", they were talking *rural development* loans. These are zero down mortgages.

I often have clients that aren't able to come up with a down payment and are either looking in outlying areas or flexible with where they would like to live. In many of these cases they have qualified for the USDA rural development loan.

The most common misconception is that you need to live in the middle of nowhere to qualify for this loan program. This is NOT TRUE. It doesn't need to be a rural farm property with cows, chickens, and an outhouse….or whatever stereotype you are probably thinking in your head! The geographic restrictions with this loan are based on census numbers that were derived many years ago. As a result there are very compelling areas that qualify for the USDA loan.

You can be considered as an applicant for the USDA program in thriving cities like Sherwood, Wilsonville and many more! The qualifications and definitions of "rural" are probably not what you think. With the possibility of zero percent down, it's definitely worth looking into.

You can even buy brand new construction homes with rural development financing!

AND you can often roll the closing costs into the purchase price! If you qualify, it's a true "no money down" opportunity.

However, RD loans do have different guidelines. There is no free lunch!

For example, their debt-to-income ratios are a little bit tighter. To find out the specifics of what you might qualify for, talk to a loan officer. I'd be happy to answer your questions!

5. Programs For US Veterans

If you have served our country in the military, there is a special loan program just for you.

In fact, this mortgage product might just be the "best" program out there for homebuyers. It's called the Veteran's Administration (VA) loan.

These mortgages are amazing for veterans because the federal government fully backs them!

Some title companies will give discounts on their fees to veterans. Homeowners' insurance companies will do this as well.

There's no down payment required for VA loans. There's no monthly mortgage insurance required for VA loans. AND the rate is subsidized by the government is often below prevailing rates!

It's amazing!!!

If you're a veteran, this is an incredible opportunity.

In fact, I just did a $250,000 loan using the VA program the month before I wrote this chapter. My client put just $1,500 down in earnest money.

(When you get the contract, you put a small amount of money down to hold the house. This is called *earnest money*. Basically, this proves to the seller that you are a serious buyer. Once earnest money is put down, the house cannot publicly stay on the market. No marketing or showings are allowed for the listing.)

This cost him just fifteen hundred dollars. After everything was said and done, he got the $1,500 back at closing!

He literally paid ZERO DOWN to buy his home.

A VA loan is an incredible option for those who have served our country and if you have 10% or more disability you qualify for additional benefits. Make sure to let your loan officer know the specifics surrounding your military discharge.

Similar to FHA, it's fairly easy to qualify for a VA loan (assuming of course that you're a veteran). It's backed by the federal government, which means the stipulations and requirements are relaxed.

The federal government wants to give back to the men and women who have served our country. They fought for the American dream, so it's only fair they get to experience it for themselves!

You might be wondering...are VA loans common?

Is it really that easy for a veteran to buy a house with this program, or is it a yearlong process full of complicated paperwork and stressful qualification requirements?

The answer is simple: YES, these loans are very common for veterans. And YES, they are easy to process.

In fact, these are my absolute favorite loans to help homebuyers with.

If you have served our country, this is an amazing opportunity for Uncle Sam, and the rest of us to say, *"Thank You for Your Service!"*

A Quick Summary Of Financing Strategies

Most people automatically think, "I have to put 10 percent down or 20 percent down. And it's going to be a 30-year fixed rate."

Well, this isn't always the case!

There is a lot of flexibility….*even if you don't have the money for a big down payment.*

If you don't qualify for down payment assistance and you haven't saved enough money, you aren't automatically out of luck. You still have some options.

Getting a gift is one alternative. Do you have a generous friend or relative? A gift can be used for the down payment.

Another option that many people use is a loan against their 401k investment account. You don't get penalized for using this capital when you're buying a home.

(All you have to do is to show a copy of your purchase agreement, and the lender will loan you a certain amount of your 401K…without any withdrawal penalties.)

It's pretty cool how this works: you are actually withdrawing the money from your 401k and then paying the interest back to yourself.

I know a lot of people who have used this strategy.

You need to have some skin in the game when you are buying a house. Fortunately, with all of the programs out there for homebuyers, "skin in the game" doesn't automatically mean 20% down...*like it used to!*

REMEMBER: with rural development and VA loans, you don't have to have any money down. These are true zero down mortgage programs.

I hope I didn't confuse you with all of the various loan strategies and mortgage programs (there are lots more that I haven't even covered). Here's what you need to remember: you have **options**, and its important to work with a trusted loan officer that can explain the pros and cons of each and show you specifically the programs that you qualify for. It is all about finding the best program for YOU – for your unique and specific needs – not just putting you into a "one size fits all" program.

Chapter 4

How To Drive Your Loan Officer Crazy: The Most Frustrating Mistakes Homebuyers Make Before Closing

In this chapter, I want to share with you the most frustrating mistakes homebuyers make. These mistakes can drive loan officers absolutely crazy, because they can ruin a deal that everyone involved has spent many hours working on.

Of course, it's usually not the client's fault. It's really the loan officer's fault, *because it's the loan officer's responsibility to educate their client.*

And that's why I'm writing this chapter! I want to empower you with knowledge ahead of time, so you can avoid these costly mistakes.

So what should you NOT do before closing?

Mistake #1: Having your credit pulled multiple times.

This is very common. And, unfortunately, it WILL lower your credit score.

So, what does it mean to have your credit "pulled?"

This is mortgage industry jargon for a *credit inquiry.*

Anytime you apply for credit of any kind, the lender "pulls" your credit and makes an inquiry to check your profile.

There's nothing inherently wrong with this; however, it obviously proves that you are applying for credit. Lenders don't want to see a bunch of recent inquiries, because this can be correlated with financial *desperation.*

So, here's the game plan when buying a house:

- DON'T open credit cards.
- DON'T shop around with a bunch of different mortgage companies (they might pull your credit to start the process). *If you do interview a few loan officers, be very clear with them that you do*

NOT want them to pull your credit...until you've firmly decided to work with them.

- Don't buy a car.
- Don't apply for other loans or "credit" of any kind.

No one "needs" to look at your credit report until you've actually started the mortgage process.

If you're just researching and interviewing different loan officers, inquiries will damage your score *and make it harder to buy a home.*

You do have a little bit of leeway when you're looking for a mortgage, because the credit bureaus will give you a window of maybe two or three weeks to look around. The specifics differ for each client.

However, you don't want ten mortgage companies pulling your credit...this will definitely hurt your credit score.

You really want to be careful when you see anything resembling a credit application during the home buying process. If you're not sure if an application you're filling out might affect your credit score, CALL YOUR LOAN OFFICER.

Trust me—a quick two-minute phone call will save you a lot of stress.

For example, you do not want to have a car company looking at your credit. They do not have what's called a soft pull.

A "soft pull" is a credit inquiry that doesn't affect your official credit score.

I won't get into the boring details, but here's what you need to know: it's very, very rare that a credit inquiry doesn't affect your official credit score.

Even looking at a mortgage will affect your credit score if the loan officer "pulls" your credit (or you fill out a credit application online).

My advice? Don't take the risk. Find a loan officer you trust, and follow their lead.

Mistake #2: Buying ANYTHING With Financing.

Why is this a mistake? Won't some credit history help your credit score?

The short answer is NO.

When you buy a home, we look at your credit in the beginning of the process, and also at the very end of the process. We check to make sure that no new debt has been incurred.

This time span can be months apart, depending on how long the process takes from when you first begin looking to when you close on the home you chose.

The lender will pull a non-score report the day they draw final loan docs to make sure no new debt was established. If any new inquiries show up they will request a credit supplement to ensure no new payments need to be factored into your debt-to-income ratios.

You do not want to risk the closing of your new home on something that can wait until after everything is DONE!

I had a client recently that was in the process of buying a new home. I reviewed all the rules with him. We went over the do's and don'ts. He knew that he shouldn't make any purchases between the time of application and the time of closing.

Despite that, he bought a car with a $300 monthly payment!!!!

Yikes.

Unfortunately, this $300/mo pushed his back-end ratio over qualifying levels and prevented him from closing on the loan. Now he is living "in his car" because he didn't qualify to buy his house any more.

I don't want to be insensitive, but....*what a stupid decision!*

It was extremely frustrating for me, his real estate agent, and everyone else involved in the process. We spent hours and hours working on his application to make sure everything would go smoothly. And even though I specifically told him to not make ANY financed purchases, he chose to anyway.

And this decision prevented him from buying a home. It happens and there's really no "do overs" to immediately restore his qualifying situation.

It doesn't matter how low the payments are, the lender is looking at the "big picture" of your financial situation. Even if your debt-to-income ratio is still acceptable, the additional debt and credit inquiry from a car purchase *will* affect your credit score. DON'T RISK IT!

So if you're thinking about buying a house, *don't even think about buying a car.*

And this doesn't just apply to vehicles. It includes any other purchases you might "finance."

Whether that's a car, new appliances, T.V., furniture, jewelry, whatever you want to buy on credit......just wait!

It sounds obvious, but I'm sure you'd rather have a new home than a TV, a new oven, or couch.

You'll need a house to put all those purchases in!

So, please, once you start the home buying process, do NOT finance any purchases. Limit yourself to what you can afford to fully pay for up front, with cash.

Mistake #3: Changing Jobs In The Middle Of The Home Buying Process

Some people switch jobs because they think, "I'll earn more money at this new position, so maybe I can qualify to buy a larger house!"

While a person might be earning more money, their new job may be commission-based or include bonus income or deferred comp. This is a big no-no if you're trying to qualify for a mortgage!

Recent commission earnings or other compensation types that haven't been earned over the past 24 months can't be used in the loan process. If you get a new job that goes from salary to commission, *even if you're making more money than your previous job*, you are essentially unemployed from the lender's perspective.

Or let's say you are salaried, and your loan officer has assured you that you will qualify for the mortgage you'll need to finance your new home.

All of a sudden, you think to yourself, "I don't want to work on a salary anymore. This career isn't fulfilling. I'm going to get a job in a totally new line of work, and try something different."

While finding a more fulfilling job might be a great move for your personal life and career, *it will destroy your chances of buying a home.*

You're not going to qualify for a mortgage anymore, because you need a two-year history of consistent income (which includes type).

This happened once to a client of mine here in Portland. He was devastated when he discovered he wouldn't qualify to buy a home.

Even though I told him to wait, he foolishly decided to switch jobs anyways. He thought he was making a brave decision by "following his heart" towards a career he was more passionate about.

Unfortunately, the lender wasn't concerned about his feelings or his career aspirations. They just wanted to make sure he had consistent employment and income so he would be able to make the payments on his mortgage! Banks are pessimistic by nature and most often look at things as worse case. So despite the income potential being possibly higher – the lender looked at this scenario as not having any history of commission, therefore there was no assurance that the commission would continue. They declined the loan.

So when YOU are in the process of applying for a loan, keep your income consistent. Do NOT switch jobs.

Here are some additional tips to keep your credit score strong....

Do not use credit cards excessively. Don't max them out, and always pay them back in full every month (don't just make the "minimum payment"). A good rule of thumb is to not spend more than 30 or 40% of your credit limit. This is called the *credit utilization rate.* Spending too much on a credit card can signal that you aren't financially secure. If you can get your balances down below 15% it actually increases your scores.

Do not spend the money you have set aside for closing. If you think your closing costs will be about $3,000—and you only have $5,000—do not spend the "extra" money on a vacation. You might be short on cash if there's a surprise right before closing that you didn't anticipate. If the closing cost ends up being $3,800 and you only have $3,000 available, this is not a good situation to be in!

Never put yourself in a position where you are scrambling for money. Not only is this not a good idea from a financial perspective, it's harmful for your *emotional health.*

People that live paycheck to paycheck are more stressed than those that don't. One of the fastest ways to be a happier person in general is to have the peace of mind knowing you have "margin." Breathing room!

So save your money! Always have a safety cushion of cash.

Do not pay off major debts or liabilities without checking with your loan officer first. And NEVER ever pay off a debt and close the account.

This might sound counterintuitive, but sometimes it does more harm than good!

Let's look at an example.

Say you have a collection account and it's been active since 2007. Eight years later, it's 2015. You think, "Oh, there's a collection on my report. That's bad. I want to pay it off and close it out!"

If you don't first talk to your loan officer, here's why this might be a bad idea: often times they're not actively reporting that debt.

If you start the process of paying that off, they will start actively reporting the monthly debt….and it will count against you and the derogatory credit history will begin negatively affecting your scores again!

Even if you've paid it off, it's now on the record again.

So, in some instances, as crazy as it sounds, paying off debt can actually hurt you.

I know…it doesn't make any logical sense!

That's why you MUST talk to your loan officer before making any financial decisions throughout this process.

Do not change banks in the middle of the process.

If you're thinking about closing on a home in the next two months and you're banking with Wells Fargo, don't switch to US Bank two weeks before closing.

Stay with Wells Fargo (or whatever bank you're using) even if you hate their guts. Just wait it out. Don't deposit anything unusual into your account. Anything that's not a payroll deposit coming from your payroll, we have to *source.* This is where it will feel like the lender is the FBI and they are trying to find nefarious activities hidden in your bank account that will incriminate you. That's not the case – but because of much higher federal scrutiny on mortgage lending, it can feel like it. I can't stress enough the importance of finding a loan officer that you really trust, that has years of experience (through the good and the bad) and that is looking out for YOUR best interest not theirs. They will help guide you through this process in the most efficient manner possible.

Imagine that your brother owed you $500, and he just feels now is the time to pay you the $500....don't put it in your account. Or maybe you won a bunch of money from the casino....don't put it in your account.

We cannot trace that. We can't use that money. You cannot trace cash. This is what it means to "source." We need to be able to trace the money!

So don't put cash into your account.

Obviously, there's a good reason for this. Regulators and lenders will wonder, "Well, where'd that money come from?"

The bank is probably thinking, "Is this person dealing drugs? Did they rob a bank to get the money? Are they running an illegal prostitution syndicate?"

Whether these suspicions are based on correlation (rather than causation) is irrelevant....*just don't do it!* Don't make unusual cash deposits that cannot be sourced.

To be completely honest, they probably don't care where you got it. *It's more of a business decision than a moral safeguard.* However because real estate transactions became a hotbed for money laundering leading up to the "crash", new federal regulations require lenders to "snoop around" more.

The lender can usually assume it's simply not sustainable if you have random $200 cash deposits, $900 cash deposits, etc. This is not how "normal" people with steady, reliable jobs operate. And therefore, it's a red flag for lenders and possible federal oversight.

Don't cosign for anything, ever.

This will go against your debt-to-income ratio, because you ARE liable for that payment.

For example, if you have a daughter who wants a car and she doesn't qualify on her own, it's better for you to give her money to buy her own car (versus cosigning on a loan for her), because that loan is in your name.

Just because you're not making the payments doesn't mean you aren't liable for the loan.

It will count against your *debt to income* ratio, even if your daughter is perfectly responsible and makes all the payments by herself. This is a general rule of thumb to go by. If you have already cosigned on a loan we should discuss all the particulars and what your options are.

Don't "take your time" getting documentation to your loan officer.

They're not 'bugging' you because they think it's fun to harass you at work. When your loan officer asks you for documents (paychecks, last year's taxes, etc), *it's because they need it….. ASAP.* Remember the attorney analogy? Your loan officer is your advocate. Most often the underwriter is requesting additional documentation based on questions that came up from the original submission. The more you give upfront, the easier it is for the underwriter to approve the loan.

If it takes you days and/or weeks to get them what they need, *your loan will not close on time,* and you might not be able to buy the house! A responsible and experienced loan officer will request your income and asset documentation at the time of application – and often will require this documentation to validate your pre-approval. Delays in getting requested documentation is the single BIGGEST reason why loans don't close on time.

The following are minimum documentation requirements for pre-approval and submission to underwriting:

1. Most current 2 yrs W2s
2. Most current 2 yrs filed federal tax returns with all schedules
3. Most current 30 days paystubs
4. Most current 2 months asset statements ALL pages (checking, savings, 401k, IRA, stocks, etc.)

If you own 25% or more of a business; if you pay or receive child support; if you have a previous bankruptcy or foreclosure; or if you are military applying for a VA loan there will be additional documentation requirements. Make sure to discuss with your loan officer.

Chapter 5

A Simple Formula To Buy Your Dream Home (Why You Shouldn't Automatically Trust Online Mortgage Calculators)

Let's talk about finding your dream home.

Obviously, there's not a surefire formula that will spit out to the penny what you'll qualify for. There are too many variables that will affect your credit, how much money you need for a down payment (which will effect the monthly payments), etc.

However, there *is* a general formula that can get you started so you know what to expect (and can start budgeting accordingly).

If you already own a home and you're thinking about upgrading to the next level, this process will help you plan things out also. Maybe you currently own a

$200,000 home, and you've been eyeing one that's $350,000.

That's your *dream home*. That's the home that you want to raise your family in, and own it for 30 years or 40 years. That's the house you want your kids to remember as their "childhood home."

I want to go through some of the practical things you can do right now to set yourself up to buy that dream home.

In the time since you bought your last house (usually 5-10 years for most "move up" buyers), you probably received some sort of pay increase. Therefore, your income is going to be higher....*which creates a more favorable debt to income ratio.*

Ultimately, everything flows back to the DTI ratio. If you make enough to qualify for a new mortgage payment plus the debts that you hold right now, then you can afford that $350,000 house. *If you don't, you'll know exactly what the marginal difference is.*

The DTI ratio is the most important determinant in the home buying equation.

To find out the potential payment on your $350,000 dream home, you can go online and use a mortgage calculator.

However, they're usually not perfectly accurate. Most online mortgage calculators don't take into consideration homeowner's insurance, property taxes, mortgage insurance, etc.

To be fair, this is usually "user error." Most users are not entering in all the debts they have (and the aforementioned expenses). They don't know what to put in, and they miss things.

These online calculators are also prone to miscalculating the interest rate. In almost every case, the default rate in the placeholder text is *too good to be true.*

The interest rate varies on so many things – including one day to the next!

Almost always, it's going to be higher than quoted. It's classic bait and switch advertising. They catch prospective homebuyers hook, line, and sinker. They hook you in with a low *prime* rate to get you excited, and then they capture your contact information. With enough follow up (and phone sales scripts), they convert you into a customer.

Once you get started, you'll find out that the actual interest rate is much higher than you were "quoted."

So, really, online mortgage calculators aren't as helpful as people think. The main variable of your mortgage is your overall credit situation, NOT the advertised interest rates. The latter depends on the former.

Two similar people might qualify for completely different mortgage terms.

Just because your neighbor got their mortgage at 5 percent doesn't mean that you deserve 5 percent. It's completely dependent on your current financial situation. You may qualify for 4.625% because your situation is different....or maybe you'll qualify for 5.5%.

You might be looking at houses in the same neighborhood, you might have gone to the same college, maybe you even work at the same company! None of that matters—what you qualify for is determined on an individual, case-by-case basis.

The fastest way to find out exactly how much you qualify for, and exactly what price range you should be looking in, is to talk to a loan officer. A compentant loan officer can help you begin budgeting for your new home by giving you realistic numbers based upon your unique and individual circumstance.

Chapter 6

What To Expect The First Time You Talk With A Loan Officer

Let's say you own a $200,000 house.

You might not know if you qualify for $380,000 or $325,000 to buy your dream home....*talk to a loan officer.*

Loan officers are not scary. We won't bite!

People are very intimidated by loan officers because they have to show them their personal finances and their credit history.

Sometimes they have things in their finances or credit history that they're not proud of.

Sometimes they've been shunned or looked down on by other people because of past financial mistakes, so they're embarrassed.

A great loan officer is going to look at you as an *awesome* client, regardless of your past. They're going to say, "This is great! I'm so glad you contacted me. I can't wait to help you become a homeowner!"

You will be able to sense the enthusiasm in their voice. A great loan officer has a natural sense of energy— maybe "joy" is the right word—when it comes to helping people buy homes.

To a great loan officer, it's more than a job. It's a mission. Almost a *calling.*

They're going to educate you on how to get your credit scores up, how much money you'll need to make, how to optimize your debts, etc, so you can buy your dream home.

As I advised earlier, if you learn nothing else from reading this book, it's that the most important decision you make when buying a home is finding a real estate professional that you TRUST.

Ask for testimonials. Ask to talk to their clients. Look at their personal website or Facebook page. Do they have a lot of closings? Do they speak with authority? Do they have empathy towards their clients, or do they just treat them like statistics?

If the loan officer does their due diligence, they will ask questions like:

- Do you have a bankruptcy?

- What's your current job status?

- Have you had a foreclosure?

The loan officer should ask these questions early on, because the answers to these questions will determine the rest of the process.

They might ask you for documentation to verify your income. For example, if you verbally state that you make $4,500/month, they may ask you for recent paychecks to prove it.

It's a good idea to ask them before you meet, "Are there any documents you'd like me to bring to our meeting?"

This will show the loan officer that you are proactive, and that you are serious about buying a home!

A great loan officer won't be overzealous in wanting to pull your credit score, until they first get a contextual understanding of your financial situation by *actually talking with you*.

If you haven't had a recent bankruptcy, you have some liquid funds saved up for a down payment, and you have verified your employment status, THEN the loan officer should ask, "OK, great! I'll need to look at your credit report to determine what you're going to qualify for. Is that okay?"

They will explain to you why they want to view your credit, and the implications.

Usually, credit reports are good for 90 or 120 days.

If you're meeting with a loan officer for the first time and in the first 10 minutes they immediately want to "pull" your credit, don't let them do it. You should get to know them a little bit more before you allow them to make an official credit inquiry.

TIP: DO NOT LET ONLINE MORTGAGE AGGREGATORS PULL YOUR CREDIT! These are the Lending Tree, BankRate.com, Quicken and Pay My Bills websites that sell all of your information to literally dozens and dozens of internet lenders. This is opening up so many cans of worms.... Depending on how many credit inquiries result from this process – you can be looking at severely damaged credit. At minimum you will get inundated by phone calls from telemarketers trying to hard sell you on their "too good to be true" rates and your mailbox heretofore will be FILLED with new junk mail.

There aren't strict legal or ethical guidelines for this situation, so you're going to need to use your instinct and common sense.

Sometimes clients walk into my office and say, "I want to get pre-approved."

I'll politely respond, "OK, what's your situation?" They tell me, and then I ask if I can view their credit report.

I always *ask for permission* before pulling a credit report.

A good loan officer will always honor that.

A loan officer can't just say, "What's your social security number" and then make a rushed credit inquiry. Once you trust them, you should give them permission. Go with your gut.

What To Look For When Meeting With A Loan Officer

Make sure the company is reputable. Look them up. Make sure they have a good standing with the *Better Business Bureau*.

That's huge.

Make sure they've been around for a while, and they're not just a three-year company. They need to be able to stand up for their reputation. When the housing boom got into full swing, many mortgage companies popped up wanting a piece of the action. Today, some of them aren't around anymore.

Make sure you work with a lender with *a proven reputation.*

Again, ask for testimonials. This is the easiest and fastest way to evaluate a lender.

"Do you have any testimonials from any of your previous clients?" See what they say. Look them up on LinkedIn. Look them up on Facebook. What does their company website look like? Do they have a personal/business website? Those channels are easy to do research on, and they will reveal a lot!

You don't need to spend weeks researching. You should be able to look up testimonials and research your loan officer on social media in less than an hour or two. Don't spend too much time on this—but don't skip it altogether, either.

Many times, your agent is going to have an existing relationship with the loan officer. Listen to what your agent says. If you trust your agent, it's a good sign that you can probably trust their recommendation. You should still research the LO they recommend, but the agent's willingness to refer is usually a good indicator.

Why, you ask? Their reputation is on the line!

If an agent works with a loan officer that pre-approves without due diligence, deals WILL fall apart—and that makes the real estate agent look bad.

Most agents are VERY selective in which loan officers they recommend. So while you should still cross-reference their recommendations, you'll have peace of mind knowing that their incentives are aligned with your own – to ensure that you get your home!

Chapter 7

Two Real-Life Stories That Prove Honesty Is Always The Best Policy

I would like to share a few REAL stories from REAL Oregonians who didn't get pre-approved.

(I've changed the names, details, and specific locations to protect their identities)

I had a client that was referred to me by one of my best agents. She said that she'd been talking to this guy for a while, and that he was ready to buy a house. She wanted him to get a pre-approval letter before she spent time running around to view different properties.

I called him up to start the process. He was a business owner, and he was very adamant about not looking at his credit. I explained the importance of reviewing his credit not only from a qualifying score standpoint, but also to ensure there were no errors on his report that could hold things up. It happens more than you might think.

He was in Tigard actually (where my current office is). He was a very successful businessman, so I assumed that his income was going to be what he said it was.

It was—he had very strong income!

I asked him all the relevant questions a loan officer should ask: bankruptcies, foreclosures, divorces?

"Oh, yeah, I have been divorced."

Do you have kids? "Yes, I do."

Do you pay child support and/or alimony? "No, I don't."

I asked, "Okay, great. You don't pay child support?"

He said, "I don't have to."

(Some divorced parents don't have to pay child support. They just have a 50-50 agreement without an official payment requirement)

Confident that he would qualify, he went out with the agent to look at some houses. They were awesome houses. After some searching, we found a beautiful home for $320,000.

He had plenty reserved for the down payment, which is usually a very good sign!

I was able to confidently tell him, "Okay, great. I have verified your credit, your scores are great and everything looks good—we will definitely be able to get this done."

He had an 800 credit score!!!

800 is an amazing credit score...that's almost unheard of these days!

BUT...

He had a $680 child support payment, and an $820 alimony payment.....*that he didn't tell me about.*

That's a lot of money. It's also something that is clearly asked on the mortgage application. These figures may not show up on tax returns – we only truly know after a preliminary title report and judgment search is ordered after a buyer is in contract.

That's $1,500 a month in liabilities he didn't mention!

As a result, he didn't qualify for the house that he wanted. He was devastated.

When his real estate agent heard the news, she frantically called me at 9PM.

"What happened? Oh my Gosh. I thought..."

All I could tell her was, "Based upon what he had told me and the application information..."

The only "warning sign" this client showed was an extreme hesitance of me looking up his credit. Of course, I notified the agent right away when this happened.

When someone doesn't want you to look up their credit, they are usually trying to hide something. But in this case, all of the "surface" signs were looking good.

He had strong income, and a great reputation because of his successful business.

I gave him a pre-approval based on the credit report I finally talked him into allowing me to open, the income I looked at, tax returns, and other documentation.

Minus the most recent year's tax returns that weren't filed yet, it was a normal pre-approval.

The agent had known this homebuyer for years, and really trusted that he was being honest.

As a loan officer, I had reservations. I told her that he had major, major payments. And it's never a good sign when someone doesn't want you to look up their credit!

Well, it turned out that he wasn't able to buy the house. He was livid.

But it was no one's fault but his own. I asked him if he had child support. He said no. The mortgage application specifically asks if the borrower has child support and/or spousal obligations.

Moral of the story?

It's always in your best interest to be honest. As we all learned as kids, *honesty is always the best policy.*

If you're hiding something, hoping that it won't be found out, well, trust me....the loan officer WILL find out. And the further along you are in the homebuying process, the more painful it will be!

Another shocking experience involved the CEO of a sizable company that made a strong income.

Unfortunately, her husband was laid off. Even so, she qualified for the home and everything was fine. I got through the full approval process.

But here's what she didn't tell me: she was pregnant.

Later on in the process, she made the decision to go on maternity leave. We could have used her income during these few months.

But then she went on extended, *unpaid* maternity leave. And that turned out to be the reason we couldn't qualify her.

Here's the crazy part: if she would have bought the house a week earlier, everything would have been fine.

Now, let me be clear: *there is nothing wrong with going on maternity leave.*

But because she wasn't making her full monthly income on the extended unpaid maternity leave, and her husband was on unemployment income (which doesn't count), her debt-to-income ratio didn't qualify.

This is a good teaching point—not being able to buy a house doesn't mean you are a failure. In this case, the woman was a CEO! She made a great income, and had a dynamic, successful career.

She didn't make an error that ended up in job loss, she didn't have a bankruptcy, she didn't rack up wild credit card debts, or make any of the stereotypical financial mistakes that society judges people for.

In fact, most people would look up to her as a role model for how to manage your personal finances.

But one "little" mistake messed the process up. The mistake was simply withholding information. Had this been discussed openly, the loan officer could manage the situation and help advise accordingly.

The good news? She *did* buy the house.

She had to wait a month till she was back at work and had "income consistency." Fortunately, the home was still available after this waiting period.

We had to get a letter from her HR department stating she was back at work full time. She did buy the house, but it was EXTREMELY stressful for everyone involved.

Moral of the story?

Do not make any decisions that are going to affect your regular, steady, consistent monthly income, OR monthly debt.....without first talking to your loan officer.

It's the ratio that matters (DTI ratio).

On the *income* side of things, don't go on maternity leave that's unpaid...or quit your job entirely!

On the *debt* side of things, don't go buy a $2,000 big-screen TV and finance it....even if it's a special "zero percent" financing promotion.

Use common sense, and ALWAYS TALK TO A LOAN OFFICER BEFORE MAKING ANY FINANCIAL DECISIONS. When in doubt make the call that can make the difference between happy homeowner and NO HOME FOR YOU!

Chapter 8

Why A Pre-Approval Gives You A HUGE Advantage Over Other Buyers (Especially In A Seller's Market)

In the early 2000's housing boom, many real estate agents were not requiring a pre-approval. The market was so hot, they didn't want to waste valuable time getting someone pre-approved.

They simply assumed everyone would qualify (and because of the relaxed standards at the time, most people did). Maybe you heard the credo back then, "we lend to anyone that can fog a mirror." Sounds a bit comical, but certainly wasn't far from the truth.

So...why do most agents today require a pre-approval?

Well, it's because the lender guidelines and requirements are different; very different! The banks are not as lenient as they were during the housing boom.

They're not just giving loans out like candy. They're taking steps to ensure we don't have another housing bubble—and that means being stricter on who does and doesn't qualify for a mortgage.

What many people don't realize is that it costs a real estate agent money to work with a client.

And they need to front that expense until they get a commission check. Well, *if* they get a commission check (it's a big IF).

This is why real estate agents are careful who they work with. If they don't think you're actually a serious buyer, they won't want to spend money to work with you. They only want to work with serious buyers *that will actually qualify to buy a house.*

That's something most people don't think about!

All of the miles (and time) spent driving around can really add up. Many agents will drive 30,000-40,000 miles a year. Sometimes over 50,000!

They drive all over the state.

Can you imagine wasting all those miles, energy, and time away from your family? Missing soccer games, dance recitals, whatever the case may be.

Imagine having your husband frustrated, or your wife frustrated, because you're gone all the time. And then you find out that the time was wasted on someone that didn't even qualify *because they lied to you about their financial situation!*

In the aftermath of the housing boom, agents have wised up. They want to make sure that their buyer clients are qualified, right from the get-go. They are doing their due diligence to protect not only their resources, but as we mentioned before, their reputation also and everyone's time.

So if you're going to buy a house in a seller's market, being pre-approved is a competitive advantage!

Think about it. Imagine that you're selling your house, and you have two interested buyers.

Let's say the house is $250,000, and the first buyer is offering $260,000....because they really want this house. The other buyers are coming in at the original listing price, $250,000.

Naturally, you think, "OK, I'm going to take the $260,000! Sweet!"

Wait a minute—are these buyers qualified for that amount? If you accept their offer, will they actually be able to close on the house?

After asking some questions, you find out that the buyers who offered $250,000 are pre-approved for that amount, but the buyers who offered $260,000 haven't even started the qualification process.

What will you do? **What *should* you do?**

If you're smart, you'll take the lesser offer, *because it will actually close.*

Being pre-approved versus prequalified can actually give you a competitive advantage in the buying process. In a situation like this, you'll be able to win a bidding war with less money than your competitors, because the confidence you give the sellers is worth much more than the empty promise of an unqualified offer.

And just so you know, this happens ALL THE TIME.

This is not a rare thing, or an isolated incident. It is very common for buyers to "win the deal" because of their initiative in arranging financing *before* house hunting. It's also important to encourage the seller and/or seller's agent to call your loan officer to discuss your pre-approval. This shows you are both serious and ABLE.

When buying a home, it's the ultimate competitive advantage. *Especially in a seller's market* where there are multiple offers and bidding wars on limited inventory.

For example, there's a large bank here in Portland. It's nationwide, but I won't go into the details on which specific bank it is. Their pre-approvals and pre-qualifications are garbage, and agents know this.

This bank does NOT do proper due diligence with its clients – they simply rely on the fine print in their "pre-approval" letter that covers their backside. Many real estate agents I know have been burned enough to realize that they shouldn't trust buyers that are using this particular lender.

I don't need to go into who it is. The bottom line is they aren't doing their job to truly *qualify* buyers.

A lender should not be a PR firm, trying to advertise their clients as being perfect, regardless of the truth. They should be more like an investigative agency that does its due diligence in researching clients.

If the truth isn't good enough, they should fix it—not cover it up.

Here's a true story from some clients I recently worked with in Salem. They lost bidding wars on three beautiful houses in the $300,000 range.

The wife was pregnant throughout this process. It was a stressful time for them!

As they were making offers, they came from the perspective that it was a buyer's market, when really it was a seller's market.

They were not making their offers high enough, relative to the demand, often asking for concessions or even price reductions.

The agent gently advised that they needed to adjust their offers, but they were just not willing to do it.

Well, it obviously wasn't working! They had lost out on three houses. By the fourth house, they ended up going in right at the purchase price.

The list price was $303,000. They offered $303,000 with no concessions. Another person came in at $308,000, with an approval from the infamous bank I mentioned earlier.

As he should have, the seller's agent cautioned them on taking the higher offer, because of the potential problems they might have faced when it came time to actually close the deal.

Unlike the other buyers, my clients had been through the approval process, with a solid pre-approval.

Even though they had received a higher offer, the sellers called within 25 minutes of our offer to accept it.

My buyers were ecstatic.

They couldn't believe it. They quickly asked, "What was the reason that you accepted ours?

(My buyers had found out that there was a higher offer)

The sellers simply replied, "Because it was a credible approval, and we trusted you would actually be able to qualify to buy our house."

Chapter 9

The Number One Rule Of Mortgages

I would like to take a moment to talk about the number one rule of mortgages. More appropriately asked is, what is the number one rule of GETTING a mortgage?

What is this rule you ask?

Well, I suppose it's kind of a trick question. While there are too many rules in mortgage lending to even begin counting (there are literally thousands of pages of legislation regulating the mortgage industry - the Dodd-Frank Consumer Protection Act, Home Mortgage Disclosure Act and the Real Estate Settlement Procedures Act just to name a few)....There really is ONLY one thing to consider in GETTING a mortgage.

#1 – MOST IMPORTANT

START with a loan officer you can TRUST.

Buying a house is an open-ended process with many variables and lots of moving parts. This is not a one-variable or a two-variable game. There are literary dozens of variables that go into whether or not you qualify, how much you'll qualify for, what your interest rate will be, etc.

Every situation is unique. To find a constant in this sea of variables, to find one thing that stands true in every situation, it's simple: work with a loan officer you can trust.

So why should people trust *me*, Tony Gillard?

People trust me because I've been in the industry for over 12 years. I have great customer testimonials that I'm willing to publicly share with any of my clients including several Realtors and Title that have used me for their own personal transactions.

I have experience helping clients secure loans through Veterans Administration, Rural Development,

Conventional, Jumbos, and Federal Housing Administration (FHA).

I'm always looking out for what's in my client's best interest...*even if it's not their original plan.* I always tell my clients what they need to hear—not what they want to hear.

It's not always the easy thing to do, but it's the right thing to do.

And that's why I get so many referrals!

For example, first-time homebuyers need to work with someone who understands the tax implications and budget impact of home ownership to accurately determine a new homebuyer's actual buying power. Often times a homebuyer will qualify to buy much more home than they would be comfortable with. And in other cases when factoring in the incredible cash savings of deductible mortgage interest expense and adjusting one's withholding, the budget impact of going from a renter to an owner is manageable. But it takes an experienced and trusted loan officer to help guide you through this.

It comes back to being a teacher and an advisor....versus being a "loan salesperson."

I guide every buyer throughout the entire process, making sure to keep them updated on how things are going with consistent and frequent updates. Communication is extremely important to me! I never want my clients to wonder what is going on.

When my clients get to move in to their new home, it is a joyous occasion. Many hugs, sometimes even tears of joy and always a very gratifying experience for me!

I keep in contact with my newfound friends afterwards, and I make myself available to answer any questions that may come up. It's fun! I get to cultivate relationships, and build actual *friendships* with my clients. It's important to me that they feel comfortable using me as a resource. I take my advisor role very seriously and want to help long after the 'deal' closes.

Every quarter I send out an updated analysis of market activity in their area (homes that have sold in their neighborhood) so they can see how their property is appreciating. Also, on the anniversary of their new home, I send a market update relative to the rate on their mortgage to see if there is opportunity to save interest expense or in some cases to roll a longer-term mortgage like a 30 year into a shorter-term mortgage like a 15 year; which will not only shave years off the mortgage but will save significant interest expense over the life of the loan.

I love that. I love going to bed at night, knowing that I have truly helped someone live *the American dream and have helped manage it year after year.*

My youngest child once asked me, "Daddy, what do you do all day?"

I told her, "I help people find their way home." I love my job!

Chapter 10

What's The Lowest Credit Score I Can Have...*And Still Qualify To Buy A Home?*

Wow! This is definitely a loaded question.

Before I begin to answer it, I should acknowledge that *this is probably not a good question to ask.*

If you know your credit isn't very good, you shouldn't be worried about finding the minimum requirements, you should be diligently taking steps to improve your credit...so it's not an issue!

That being said...

People sometimes ask me, "What is the lowest credit score I can have and still qualify to buy a house?"

As with many questions in this book, the honest answer is: *it depends.*

The truth is that some people can buy a house with a 550 credit score. Some people will have to be at a 640 or higher.

The average credit score for a homebuyer is between 640 to 740.

If you're reading this and your credit score is less than 700, this doesn't mean that you'll never be able to buy a house. While your score isn't perfect, it's not necessarily "bad."

In fact, an average credit score is somewhere between 600-700.

You can still buy a house. If you have a 600 credit score, you can still qualify to purchase a home. While not guaranteed (it depends on your specific situation), it's entirely *possible.*

A score that's between 600-700 is average. It's decent. It's not *good* credit. It's certainly not *excellent* credit. "Excellent" credit, in my own estimation, is anything

720 and above. In Fannie Mae's estimation it's actually more like 740 and above.

If you're 550 and below, you'll need the help of a credit repair specialist. It's not the end of the world. You can still buy a home if you can get your score raised. If you map out a responsible plan to pay down debts, you'd be surprised how quickly you can improve your credit score!

I work with people all the time who, when they first met me, felt completely *hopeless.* They didn't realize their credit was so low. They expected a score of 650, but it was 550....or worse. They were frustrated, embarrassed, even a little angry.

But guess what?

In 6 to 12 months, we get them on a plan. We work with specialists who advise them on how to *strategically* pay down debts, and more responsibly manage their personal finances.

We get them on the path to success, and *voila!* They become homeowners.

Here's what you need to remember: it doesn't matter how low your score is. What matters if what you do when you find out your credit score.

If a loan officer pulls your credit and your score is 530, you're probably not going to be able to buy a house. But that doesn't mean you'll *never* be able to buy a house. The next step the loan officer takes will often show whether they are a trusted advisor or a loan sales person.

I have a great relationship with a credit-repair specialist that I work with. We work together to make sure that our clients have the knowledge and the tools to get their credit scores up...quickly.

A credit repair specialist is like a plumber for your finances—they'll find out what's not working, and fix it. Fixing your credit isn't as simple as "paying down your debts." You'll need to be strategic about which ones are paid down first, if at all. Sometimes it's just a waiting game, and you need more time for the positive factors in your score to gain momentum.

Here's what happens first: my credit repair specialist will review your credit report to make sure that everything is reported accurately. Sometimes creditors do not report things accurately!

They can get that removed from your credit report, and then your scores are going to jump up.

If you don't have any credit, you can start with a secured credit card.

For instance, maybe you had a bankruptcy eight years ago and you don't have any credit cards. A secured credit card will require you to put some money down (to collateralize the debt), but it will enable you to establish credit.

Here's how it works.

You give the credit card company $300 in an account, and then you have a $300 limit to be able to use that credit card and build credit.

You get gas with that card, and then you pay it down to 15% of the $300 or $45. Get groceries. Pay it down to $45. Go out to eat? Pay it down to $45.

Functionally, it's not much different than a debit card.

You just have to show them that you're making a positive payment history, building credit and then eventually it does help to raise your credit score.

You can always repair a credit score. Always.

So...how long does it take to fix troubled credit? Is repairing a credit score a 12-month process? 18 months?

Not always. Absolutely not! Every situation is different.

Some credit scores can be repaired in just one month. Some of them I can repair in less than *two weeks*. Some of them can take six months. It just depends what we're dealing with and what needs to be corrected.

That's where my credit-repair specialist would review your report and advise you. They would help you create a custom plan, *just for you*, that will put you on the path to homeownership!

And this brings us back to a key point of why I decided to write this book.....

Chapter 11

The Scariest Part About Buying A Home

I talk to a lot of clients that say, "You know what? I had a terrible, terrible experience the last time I worked with a loan officer. I'm just going to be upfront with you about that. You'll need to prove me wrong."

Challenge accepted!

I like to know that because then I know why they're so guarded when I ask them questions.

That's totally understandable.

We've all had bad relationships, whether it be with a dentist, an insurance agent, or whomever. You walk out thinking, "That was the *worst experience, ever.* I'm not going back."

For me personally, when I buy a car, I feel like I can get taken advantage of because I'm not a confrontational person. I don't do well in zero-sum negotiations where it's not a win-win (obviously when you buy a car, any money you save is "lost" by the dealer, so there's really never a win-win solution).

When I've bought cars in the past, I don't feel that I've been treated with much respect. Whether it's reality, or just an irrational fear in my head, I always feel like I'm being taken advantage of!

"We're going to charge him as much as we can. Get him to buy the warranties, the service protection plans, the oil change packages, blah-blah-blah-blah-blah."

So, the last time I bought a car, I immediately had my guard up.

When the salesman walked over, the look on my face was easy to read: *I'm just looking. I'm just looking. Leave me alone....I'm just looking.*

Eventually, another salesman came along and I told them the same thing, verbally: "Oh, I'm just looking."

But this salesman gets it.

He said to me, "I can sense that you're nervous and that you're uncomfortable being in here. Let me just assure you I'm not trying to pressure you. I'm just here if you have any questions."

This put me at ease.

He's not going to try to pressure me or hard-sell me. Finally, someone who wants to serve...not sell!

For many people, they think buying a house is going to be a similar experience to buying a car.

This is simply not true.

No one will pressure you into doing something you do not want to do. As loan officers, it's our duty to empower you to make a decision for yourself.

I want you to know you have options, but I won't pressure you to make any particular decision. My job is to provide you with all of the relevant information that you need to make the best decision for you.

That way I can relax—and YOU can relax—and we can leave those pushy sales tactics to the slick car salesmen.

No one wakes up one morning and says, "I really wish I had a mortgage!".....what they want is a HOME.

I make the process of getting a mortgage smooth and predictable so that you can focus on getting *the home of your dreams*. And, so that you smile!